Michigan

simply beautiful

BACK COVER: Ausable Point Lighthouse at Pictured Rocks National Lakeshore on Lake Superior. DARRYL R. BEERS

FRONT COVER: Pictured Rocks National Lakeshore rises over 200 feet above Lake Superior and extends about 15 miles. **(TOP)** Maple leaf in puddle with autumn reflections. MARK S. CARLSON

FRONT FLAP: Sunset reflections on Lake Superior. MARK S. CARLSON

BELOW: Big Falls on the East Branch of the Huron River. MARK S. CARLSON

RIGHT: Grazing horses near Bessemer in Gogebic County. DARRYL R. BEERS

TITLE PAGE: A winter's sunset over Crystal Lake. DARRYL R. BEERS

ISBN 1-56037-243-5

Photographs © 2003 Darryl R. Beers, Mark S. Carlson and Claudia Adams
© 2003 Farcountry Press

From the Photographers...

Mark S. Carlson

Orchids comprise the second largest family of flowering plants in the world. The small white lady's-slipper is becoming increasingly rare in its southern Michigan habitat.

The name Michigan is derived from the word *meicigama*, meaning "great water" in the native Chippewa language. With more than 38,500 square miles of Great Lakes (including 3,200 miles of shoreline), 11,037 square miles of inland lakes, and 36,000 miles of rivers and streams, Michigan's designation as The Great Lake State is very apropos. Always the lure for family vacations, our greatest natural resource became my continuing inspiration as a budding nature photographer. Growing up in the capital city of Lansing, a Great Lake was only a 2-hour drive to the east or west of my home. Soon, my search for natural beauty would lead me on repeat journeys to waterways and scenic shorelines throughout both peninsulas. This passionate vision quest began 25 years ago and happily continues to this day.

Within the boundaries of "great water" exists myriad related natural history subjects, some of which are unique to the Great Lakes region. One topic of personal affection is the enchanting beauty of native wildflowers. Our area boasts more than 60 native orchid species, second only to Florida in the entire country. Their fragile habitats often owe their very existence to the climatologic conditions created by the Great Lakes.

One pristine example is the international biosphere known as Isle Royale, Michigan's only national park. An archipelago of islands, Isle Royale is true northern wilderness emerging out of the frigid waters of Lake Superior, some 50 miles off the mainland. Home to a precariously balanced population of moose and wolves, this rugged gem of nature hosts a multitude of specially adapted flora and fauna, all thanks to its location within the largest freshwater lake in the world.

A favorite venture of mine is photographing the waterfalls of the Upper Peninsula. More than 150 of them adorn the wild rivers and streams of the rocky Upper Peninsula hill country. Translating their hypnotic seduction onto film has always been one of my most welcomed creative challenges.

Among all the natural highlights of Michigan rest some of the most charming pastoral farm scenes this side of New England. From the hip-roof barns of the "thumb" area to the rolling orchards in the "little finger" of the Leelanau Peninsula, remnants of our agricultural heritage sit like Wyeth paintings across the landscape. My ambition has always been to record as many of these vanishing links to the past as possible. In order to capture their ethereal qualities—the texture of wood and stone structures and the idyllic settings that quietly harken to simpler times—I've learned to imagine them from a painter's perspective before clicking the shutter.

Season after season, Michigan's wonderful diversity offers a never-ending array of subject matter. From the record snowfalls of the Keweenaw Peninsula to spring bogs full of insectivorous plants and orchids, our state is rich in natural history. Wildlife, such as white-tailed deer, elk, moose, black bear, and a vast assortment of birds, inhabit our fields, forests, and waters. Recently, with the advent of numerous sightings, the Michigan Wildlife Conservancy confirmed—through intensive research, including DNA analysis—that cougars still exist on both peninsulas. These are just a few reasons to support continued preservation of the ecosystems that help to define our Great Lake State and make Michigan simply beautiful.

—Mark S. Carlson

Although I presently reside in Wisconsin, my Michigan blood runs deep. I learned to appreciate the Great Lakes early on, as my family lived in St. Ignace across the street from Lake Huron. My father was a cook on the car ferries that crossed the Straits of Mackinac—the sole connecting link between the Upper and Lower Peninsulas. My fondest childhood memories center around riding the ferry boats and eating a warm slice (or two!) of my dad's freshly baked cherry pie.

The ferry boats are now long gone, replaced by one of Michigan's most enduring icons: the Mackinac Bridge. I liken The Bridge (as it is simply called by most Michiganders) to the stem of an hourglass—that narrow connecting point where two distinctly different worlds are funneled into one another. This is quintessential Michigan, the point from which the Great Lakes State radiates outward in all its splendor and magnificence.

To the north lies the rugged yet majestic Upper Peninsula, which is bordered by the greatest lake in the world, Lake Superior—the transcendent *Kitchi Gami*. The Upper Peninsula is truly nature's showcase. Consider the Porcupine Mountains, Keweenaw Peninsula, Pictured Rocks, Seney National Wildlife Refuge, Tahquamenon Falls, Bond Falls, Garden Peninsula, and Drummond Island. The list goes on. The 906 area code still covers the entire Upper Peninsula and surely is—as advertised—God's area code.

The Lower Peninsula, home to Michigan's major population centers, can nonetheless stake its own claim to nature's bounty. Hundreds of miles of Lakes Huron and Michigan shoreline offer great natural beauty as well as countless recreational opportunities. Natural areas abound on both shores of these Great Lakes and in the many parks that are spread throughout the central region of the state.

Michigan is steeped in rich traditions and history dating back 13,000 years, when humans first settled in the Lower Peninsula. Today, Michigan's cities are centers of cultural and ethnic diversity offering residents and visitors alike an array of activities, events, and celebrations.

Of course, I would be remiss in speaking of Michigan's wealth of assets if I did not include the more than 120 lighthouses—treasured icons of the legacy and history of the Great Lakes State.

As a landscape photographer, I view Michigan as my smorgasbord—a sumptuous and never-ending buffet of gourmet photographic delights. Nearly every year, in nearly every season, I return to my home state. I return because it is a wonderful place to be. If I am fortunate enough, during each visit, I will have succeeded in capturing on film another piece of the essence of my home state.

It gives me great pleasure to be able to share with you, in the pages that follow, some of my favorite images of the great state of Michigan. Enjoy and savor these morsels of the bountiful, picturesque feast that Michigan offers to all who take the time to look.

Proud to be a yooper,
Darryl R. Beers

Darryl R. Beers

Many a ship has wrecked off the coast of Sleeping Bear Dunes National Lakeshore. Sleeping Bear contains enormous piles of white sand and is a favorite among families as well as hikers. This is Petoskey Stone Shore.

ABOVE: Remote islands off the coast of Michigan showcase the solitude and beauty of nature. This is Middle Island in Lake Huron. DARRYL R. BEERS

FACING PAGE: The Grand Island East Channel Lighthouse surveys Lake Superior. Considered to be one of the nation's most endangered lighthouses, efforts are currently underway to save this historic and majestic Michigan icon. DARRYL R. BEERS

ABOVE: Statues of W. C. "Billy" Durant (founder of General Motors) and J. Dallas Dort stand in Flint. Dort and Durant created the Flint Road Cart Company in 1886.
DARRYL R. BEERS

RIGHT: Three baby raccoons hang out in a tree. Masked, but not yet bandits.
CLAUDIA ADAMS

Apple tree blossoms. Apple and cherry orchards abound in Michigan. MARK S. CARLSON

ABOVE: Middle Island Lighthouse on Lake Huron. Underwater preserves mark the graves of scores of ships that met their fate on stormy Huron. DARRYL R. BEERS

LEFT: Moonrise over Lake Huron from Sturgeon Point. Huron is 223 miles long and 183 miles wide, the third largest Great Lake. DARRYL R. BEERS

Falls on Fumee Creek in Helen Z. Lien Roadside Park. <small>DARRYL R. BEERS</small>

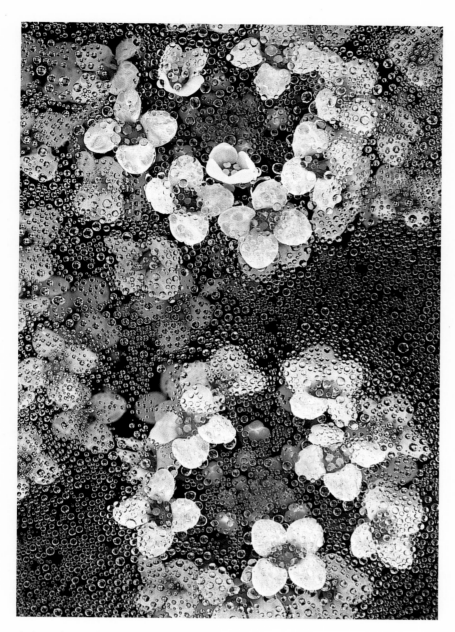

A dewy sheetweb over garden alyssum. MARK S. CARLSON

Green on black. A newly emerged luna moth on a black walnut tree. MARK S. CARLSON

LEFT: Raven's tracks in the sand. Ravens often hunt along the sand dunes of the upper Great Lakes. MARK S. CARLSON

BELOW: Weathered piling at Whitefish Point on Lake Superior. DARRYL R. BEERS

FACING PAGE: Shoreline on Drummond Island, which is part of the Manitoulin chain The island was named for a British commander who built a fort on it after it had become American territory. DARRYL R. BEERS

The Presque Isle River in Porcupine Mountains Wilderness State Park. At 92 square miles, Porcupine Mountains is the largest state park in the nation. DARRYL R. BEERS

St. Mary's Church in Phoenix. The first Jesuits came to Michigan in 1641 at the invitation of Samuel de Champlain, lieutenant governor of New France. DARRYL R. BEERS

ABOVE: A sugar maple tree at the height of its color. Leaves can begin to change color in Michigan's Upper Peninsula as early as the end of August. MARK S. CARLSON

FACING PAGE: Dawn on Isle Royale National Park, an isolated wilderness track in the northwest corner of the largest of the Great Lakes. Isle Royale is the least-visited park in the national park system. MARK S. CARLSON

LEFT: The great gray owl is the largest of all owls, but it's mostly fluff and little mass. It is usually best found in winter, when it may invade the northern United States in large numbers. CLAUDIA ADAMS

BELOW: Ice cave icicles. Which way does frozen water run? CLAUDIA ADAMS

Shoal rocks on Grand Traverse Bay on Lake Michigan. DARRYL R. BEERS

Yellow hawkweed and oxeye daisies bloom in a meadow. A weathered barn watches over the scene. MARK S. CARLSON

LEFT: The Chesaning Heritage House Restaurant in Chesaning. Chesaning means "big rock."
DARRYL R. BEERS

BELOW: A harbor at Bois Blanc Island in the north end of Lake Huron. The island has a fairly level 27-mile mountain bike loop with good views. DARRYL R. BEERS

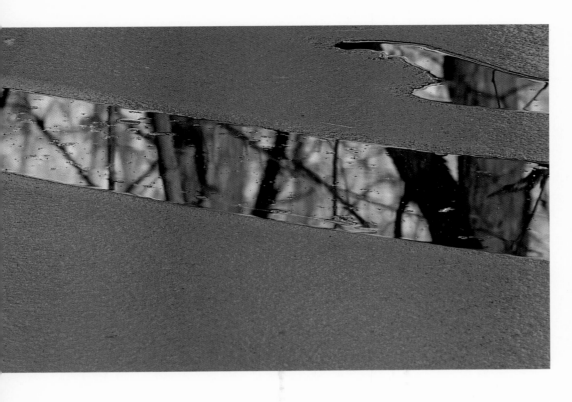

LEFT: Reflections in an icy river. MARK S. CARLSON

BELOW: Munising Falls is a five-minute walk down a paved path from the west visitor center at Pictured Rocks. The falls plummet 50 feet.
MARK S. CARLSON

White River Lighthouse at Sylvan Beach near Whitehall. The lighthouse presently houses a nautical museum where visitors can climb the tower and view the beautiful confluence of White Lake and Lake Michigan. DARRYL R. BEERS

ABOVE: The Big Carp River in Porcupine Mountains Wilderness State Park. The nine-mile Big Carp River Trail leads west from the Lake of the Clouds overlook before descending into the valley. DARRYL R. BEERS

FACING PAGE: The Tower Entrance of Beaver Head Lighthouse on the south end of Beaver Island. DARRYL R. BEERS

Shelf ice on Lake Superior
near F.J. McLain State Park.
Each winter Lake Superior's
shoreline freezes, resulting in
spectacular ice formations.
DARRYL R. BEERS

LEFT: Michigan's state wildflower, the rare dwarf lake iris, grows near the shores of the northern Great Lakes. MARK S. CARLSON

BELOW: Horserace Rapids on the Paint River in Copper Country State Forest. Stretches of the Paint River provide relatively mellow canoe rides. DARRYL R. BEERS

A fierce storm boils the water along Pictured Rocks National Lakeshore. Storms usually sweep in from the west. CLAUDIA ADAMS

Cheboygan Crib Light on Lake Huron. Originally located offshore atop a wooden crib, the decommissioned light was saved by the people of Cheboygan, who gave it a new home at the mouth of the Cheboygan River.

DARRYL R. BEERS

RIGHT: A Fancy Dress Dancer, Ira Makeshimfirst, Jr., at a powwow on Wapole Island. CLAUDIA ADAMS

BELOW: A doe seeking shelter in the woods. Around 90 percent of the Upper Peninsula is timbered; hard maple and birch are the most plentiful. CLAUDIA ADAMS

Cattails after an ice storm. MARK S. CARLSON

ABOVE: The *Highlander Sea* and *St. Lawrence II* docked at Mackinaw City. DARRYL R. BEERS

LEFT: Twelve Mile Beach on Lake Superior. Superior is the largest freshwater lake anywhere, covering 82,362 square kilometers. MARK S. CARLSON

ABOVE: The Christmas Mall in Christmas, Michigan. DARRYL R. BEERS

FACING PAGE: Winter Pond in Hiawatha National Forest. Hiawatha is the only national forest to border three Great Lakes (Huron, Michigan, and Superior). The forest consists of 46 percent wetlands and supports numerous endangered, threatened, and rare plants. DARRYL R. BEERS

ABOVE: Fireworks explode over the Detroit River during the International Freedom Festival. CLAUDIA ADAMS

RIGHT: The Fresnel Lens from the Stannard Rock Lighthouse, now on display at Marquette.
DARRYL R. BEERS

Sunset over Big Stone Creek in Wilderness State Park, 12 miles west of Mackinaw City. DARRYL R. BEERS

Marsh marigolds frequently form dense, attractive populations. These grow along Wagner Falls.

MARK S. CARLSON

ABOVE: A snowshoe hare in Isle Royale National Park. When a snowshoe changes color in winter, only the tips of the hairs turn white; beneath these is a yellowish band. MARK S. CARLSON

RIGHT: Dew on web, or is it web on dew? MARK S. CARLSON

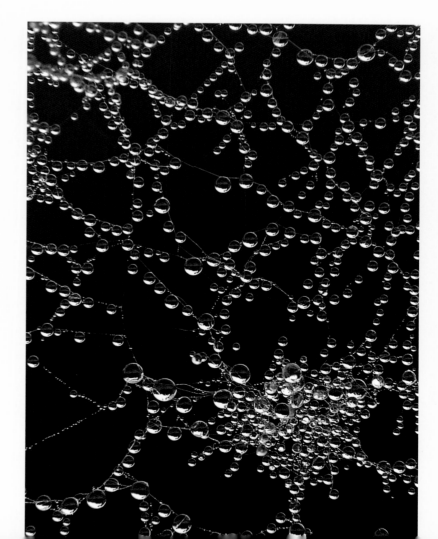

ABOVE: Red maple buds on ice. While most spectacular in autumn, the red flowers, fruit, and twigs make this tree handsome year round. MARK S. CARLSON

PRECEDING PAGES: Sunrise on Peninsula Point on Lake Michigan. Michigan has more fresh water than any other state. DARRYL R. BEERS

Winter barn near Omena. Snowplows and shovels are essential implements in Michigan. MARK S. CARLSON

A spring woodlot bisected by a creek. Spring woodland flowers must bloom
before tree leaves block sunlight from reaching the forest floor. MARK S. CARLSON

RIGHT: The painted trillium is found in moist forests and along stream banks, from the lowlands to the subalpine zone. MARK S. CARLSON

BELOW: An American toad displays its poker face.
MARK S. CARLSON

ABOVE: Daybreak on Glidden Lake in Copper Country State Forest. DARRYL R. BEERS

Upper Tahquamenon Falls is 200 feet wide and 50 feet tall and flows at 50,000 gallons per second. The water acquires a deep red from the tannin of hemlock trees upstream. DARRYL R. BEERS

LEFT: A lucky fisherman catching tiger muskie on Kingston Lake.
MARK S. CARLSON

BELOW: Lunch could be lively at the Red Dock Cafe on Kalamazoo Lake.
DARRYL R. BEERS

The Grand Haven Lighthouse endures a winter storm. Michigan has more lighthouses than any other state. CLAUDIA ADAMS

A snowbound forest in Chippewa County. Michigan has 19.3 million acres of timber, including six state forests and three national forests. DARRYL R. BEERS

A sunrise from the vantage point of Isle Royale. Boaters and experienced kayakers can travel the rocky shoreline or explore one of the many secluded natural harbors.
MARK S. CARLSON

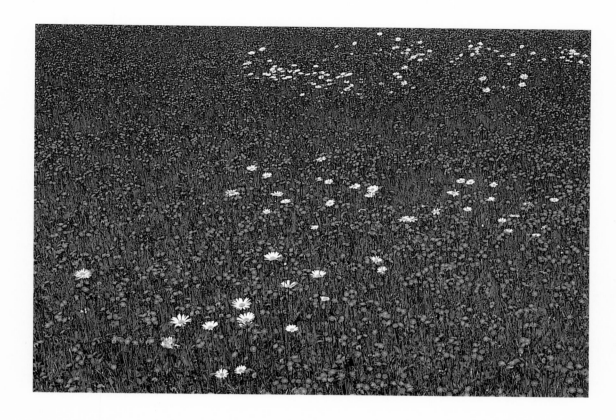

LEFT: A field of orange hawkweed punctuated with daisies.
MARK S. CARLSON

BELOW: Cardinal flowers flourish in a southern Michigan floodplain.
MARK S. CARLSON

Ludington North Pierhead Light. The pier is a popular place for tourists and locals alike to enjoy a colorful Lake Michigan sunset.
DARRYL R. BEERS

Red barn art in Alpena County along Highway 32 makes travelers smile. DARRYL R. BEERS

LEFT: Prairie coneflowers. This species produces flowers in various shades and combinations of red, brown, and yellow. MARK S. CARLSON

BELOW: Sea kayaking in Scoville Harbor at Isle Royale National Park. Isle Royale's shores are a favorite destination among sea kayakers. MARK S. CARLSON

The Rapid River in Delta County, Michigan is famous for its fall colors. DARRYL R. BEERS

LEFT: A storefront in the Old Town District of Alpena. Alpena is the primary launching point for diving excursions in Thunder Bay Underwater Preserve. Thunder Bay houses a number of shipwrecks within its boundaries. DARRYL R. BEERS

BELOW: White-tailed bucks in Sleeping Bear Dunes National Lakeshore. The largest dune in Sleeping Bear is 465 feet tall.
MARK S. CARLSON

ABOVE: Old Mission Point Lighthouse in Grand Traverse County.
The lighthouses add romance to Michigan's coasts. DARRYL R. BEERS

FACING PAGE: Windswept winter dunes on the Lake Michigan
shore. Shoreline landscapes are constantly changing. DARRYL R. BEERS

ABOVE: What most children love to experience at least once, sand baths. MARK S. CARLSON

RIGHT: Row boats at the dock at Tahquamenon Falls State Park. In addition to good rowing, the park is home to a number of unusual plant species, including the insect-eating pitcher plant. DARRYL R. BEERS

Gulls greet the day on Holland State Park Beach. Later in the morning beachgoers will arrive to laze on the waterfront. DARRYL R. BEERS

ABOVE: The misty maids of St. Joseph, pensive beauties. DARRYL R. BEERS

BELOW: Carriages will take one around Frankenmuth, which is known for its Bavarian architecture, glockenspiel towers, and festivals featuring sausages, beer, and polka music. DARRYL R. BEERS

A fallen white pine snag along Empire Bluffs in Sleeping Bear Dunes National Lakeshore. In the mid-1800s, surveyors estimated Michigan's standing pine at 150 billion board feet. MARK S. CARLSON

ABOVE: Willow tree at the mouth of Fox Creek in Menominee County. DARRYL R. BEERS

FACING PAGE: Full moon over Manistique's East Breakwater Lighthouse. DARRYL R. BEERS

RIGHT: The white-breasted nuthatch is a common bird that bounds along like a tiny woodpecker. Its long toes allow it to forage on tree trunks. MARK S. CARLSON

BELOW: White's Covered Bridge in Ionia County was built in 1867 and named after a prominent pioneer family. MARK S. CARLSON

Autumn maples reflected in a pond in Hiawatha National Forest. The forest is named for the Native American hero of Longfellow's famous poem "Song of Hiawatha." DARRYL R. BEERS

Old Mill Creek State Park in Cheboygan County. DARRYL R. BEERS

The Michigan State Capitol in Lansing. Lansing won the honor as capital in 1847 mostly because it wasn't favored by any particular party. The dome and spiral rise 267 feet.

DARRYL R. BEERS

Madeline at Heritage Harbor in Traverse City, the unofficial capital of northern Michigan. DARRYL R. BEERS

LEFT: The view from the lantern room at Old Presque Isle Lighthouse. The light could not be easily seen by ships, so another lighthouse was built a mile north. DARRYL R. BEERS

BELOW: Flowers and flags and a Michigan summer in Port Austin. DARRYL R. BEERS

The 1858 Point Betsie
Lighthouse is one of the
most photographed
lighthouses in Michigan.
DARRYL R. BEERS

ABOVE: Ancient petroglyphs in Sanilac County. About 10,000 years ago, Native Americans entered the Great Lakes region, many settling near what has become Detroit. MARK S. CARLSON

RIGHT: Collecting the sap to make the maple syrup.
MARK S. CARLSON

A road winds through flowering dogwoods. Dogwoods are one of the first trees to bloom in spring. MARK S. CARLSON

Gull Rock Lighthouse on a calm morning on Lake Superior. The lighthouse is located 2 miles off the tip of Keweenaw Peninsula. DARRYL R. BEERS

Sunset over Lake Michigan from the *SS Badger*. The *Badger* transports people and cars between Michigan and Wisconsin. DARRYL R. BEERS

RIGHT: Magnolia warblers can be difficult to observe because they often forage near the center of trees rather than at the outer edges. MARK S. CARLSON

BELOW: Fishing on the Tahquamenon Rvier in Tahquamenon Falls State Park. DARRYL R. BEERS

Staircase Falls on the East Branch of the Huron River. Michigan has about 150 waterfalls. MARK S. CARLSON

ABOVE: Red-breasted mergansers regularly mate and nest at Isle Royale National Park. They visit open coastlines during the winter. MARK S. CARLSON

LEFT: A storm approaching Great Sand Bay near Eagle River. Michigan has 3,288 miles of shoreline, more than any other state except Alaska. MARK S. CARLSON

ABOVE: Rolling cherry orchards in Leelanau County. Michigan is famous for its cherries and cherry pies. MARK S. CARLSON

Whose barn? Which cattle? In Huron County. DARRYL R. BEERS

The Quincy Mine No. 2 Shaft Hoist House is home to the Nordberg hoist, the world's largest cross-compound steam hoist, invented by Finnish immigrant Bruno V. Nordberg in 1886. It can be found near Hancock.
DARRYL R. BEERS

LEFT: A cobblestone home in Alcona County. Much of the county is covered by the Huron National Forest and resort fishing areas.
DARRYL R. BEERS

BELOW: Amway's World Headquarters in Ada, 10 miles east of Grand Rapids on the Grand River. DARRYL R. BEERS

Round Island in Lake Huron. DARRYL R. BEERS

RIGHT: Dutch Village in Holland. Holland was established in 1847 on Lake Macatawa by 54 Dutch settlers. DARRYL R. BEERS

BELOW: A pumpkin patch in Hubbardston.
MARK S. CARLSON

Daybreak at Porcupine Mountains Wilderness State Park; a series of 1,900-foot peaks make up the
Porcupines. Around 160 inches of snow falls in Michigan's mountains each year. DARRYL R. BEERS

ABOVE: A yellow-shafted flicker feather on a common evening primrose. DARRYL R. BEERS

RIGHT: There are 35 miles of lakeshore at Sleeping Bear Dunes on the northwestern coast of Michigan's Lower Peninsula. The Lower Peninsula was carved out thousands of years ago by glaciers, some 2 miles thick. DARRYL R. BEERS

St. Joseph Inner Pier Light on Lake Michigan. Lake Michigan is the world's sixth largest lake and the only Great Lake entirely within the boundaries of the United States. DARRYL R. BEERS

Evening light on winter dunes along the Lake Michigan shore near Ludington. Michigan's four seasons and abundance of water allows for many outdoor activities. DARRYL R. BEERS

RIGHT: Mushroom hunting is a popular pastime in Michigan. Black morels like this one are a favorite find. MARK S. CARLSON

BELOW: Autumn snow in a river valley in Hiawatha National Forest. Six designated wilderness areas within the forest protect wetlands, sand dunes, and timber. MARK S. CARLSON

Winter temperatures average 15 degrees F in the northern part of Michigan. MARK S. CARLSON

A couple viewing Manido Falls on the Presque Isle River. Porcupine Mountains Wilderness State Park contains 90 miles of marked hiking trails. DARRYL R. BEERS

ABOVE: Maple trees and cascades along the Whitefish River. MARK S. CARLSON

RIGHT: Large populations of red squirrels, moose, and wolves live on Isle Royale in Lake Superior. MARK S. CARLSON

Leelanau County's little red schoolhouse. Michigan is still primarily a rural state. MARK S. CARLSON

LEFT: Michigan's Upper Peninsula has experienced a resurgence in sled dog racing and guided sled dog trips. The UP's many trails and abundance of snow make it an ideal training ground. MARK S. CARLSON

BELOW: Ice shanties appear each winter in Little Bay de Noc, where northern pike can be caught. DARRYL R. BEERS

Tawas Point Lighthouse at Tawas Point State Park. The area is exceptional for bicycling. DARRYL R. BEERS

LEFT: A golden retriever plays in Lake Michigan's waves. MARK S. CARLSON

BELOW: Lake Superior shoreline near Eagle Harbor. Lake Superior has tide-like seiches directed by the winds. DARRYL R. BEERS

ABOVE: White birch and maple woods in Delta County; forests cover more than half the state. Wild shrubs droop with raspberries, currants, gooseberries, and elderberries. MARK S. CARLSON

FACING PAGE: Sunset over Lake Michigan in Mackinac County. DARRYL R. BEERS

LEFT: Spray jets through blowholes on the Lake Michigan shoreline.
CLAUDIA ADAMS

BELOW: Looking Glass River in Shiawassee County. Many of the place names in Michigan either originated from Native American words or tell something of the character of the area. MARK S. CARLSON

The freighter *Columbia Star* enters the Soo Locks at Sault Ste. Marie. The locks were begun in the 1850s to enable large ships to transport Michigan's metals. DARRYL R. BEERS

Day lilies bloom in Shiawassee County. The central region of lower Michigan is heavily farmed. DARRYL R. BEERS

RIGHT: Water lily in Lake Nettie. The weather in Michigan is typically moist and temperate, modulated by the bounty of water.
DARRYL R. BEERS

BELOW: The Jordan River is a small, fast river that cuts through a gorgeous valley. In the fall, especially, it is a favorite canoe trail.
MARK S. CARLSON

FOLLOWING PAGE: Sailing at sunset on White Lake Channel in Lake Michigan. Michigan can claim more boats than any other state. DARRYL R. BEERS